Custody of the Eyes

T0345792

Custody of the Eyes

Kimberly Burwick

Carnegie Mellon University Press
Pittsburgh 2017

Acknowledgments

Respectful acknowledgment is made to the following journals for the publication of these poems, often appearing in an earlier form:

Bellevue Literary Review: "Levi's Bicuspid Valve"
Crazyhorse: "Uncle Mengeles"
The Mississippi Review: "For Manoli Pagador in Getafe"
North American Review: "Franco's Stolen Babies," "The Catechesis, Redacted"
Ruminate: "Apace, or the Sound of Good Grasses"
Talking River: "He Flung His Arms Around His Face"
Terrain: "Like Slate Beneath Virgin's Bower," "Occhiolism," "A Way of Making April"

My sincere gratitude to the amazing folks at Carnegie Mellon: Gerald Costanzo, Cynthia Lamb and Connie Amoroso for their work on this book. Also, Stan Rubin and Beth Kanell for diligently reading earlier drafts.

Book design by Jennifer Huang

Library of Congress Control Number 2016948987
ISBN 978-0-88748-617-3

10   9   8   7   6   5   4   3   2   1

for all who have suffered under Franco's regime—
en la larga búsqueda de la verdad

and for Kevin and Levi

*Forget whistling: you have no lips for that, or for kissing the face
    of a man or a child.
Learn Latin, an it please my Lord, learn the foolish downward
    look called Custody of the Eyes.*

—Annie Dillard

*They were placed in their casket-boats
and launched, and if they couldn't swim,
whose fault was that?*

—Pattiann Rogers

Contents

I

II

III

Historical Note:

"The theft of newborns began with the Franco dictatorship in 1939. . . . The system outlived Franco's death in 1975 and continued at least through the 1980s. Some estimates put the total as high as 300,000 stolen babies."

—Sylvia Poggioli, NPR *Morning Edition*

I

Clinica San Ramon

Where cooling angels cannot
find black medic
or puncturevine, rain
brings all souls home.
Birth of each gray breath,
the tether, wholeness and glaze
of it needing muscle, flutter
and thrashing at its source,
a fragrance formed in branches
of the always tilting sycamore.
Shame you think this
when nuns come to
replace your little whisperer
with a dead freezer-baby,
all flame and barn-breath.

The Catechesis, Redacted

Smoke quilling the fleeced dirt.
I pull my hair back, no muscle
in its knotted mass. There must
be a way to think of goldenrod
as something other than death's
excess, sons and daughters in false
plywood nailed and thrown to
the distinct cooling of holy
gusts or winds so milkweed they
spin a whole field winter.
Praise in reverse, someone
slamming sentences apart in the
labor room, making arrangements
for your baby autumned
into the law of roots.

Filioque

Flint dawn, flint rise.
The feeling of feeling
nothing but geese, or the
arrival of a budding wind
on ricegrass like palm spikes
on Spanish mothers sent home
after a one cold kiss. The newborn
a factor of ghosts so watchful
they are not ghosts but a custody
of the eyes, swelling on arrival.
The womb damask and blossoming
a cache of flies.

Gauging the Three Twilights

The freezer-babies all
night long in their fathoms
of pewter like a rhapsody
I cannot take
anywhere but to civil twilight,
a devotion devoid robins,
a full everywhere of hawks,
the way calumny once cast
is always a rubble of infants, dried
lavender and goldenrod.
I scratch my scalp like a drunk
nun sailing into her transformation.
I'm asking for the return
of only six pounds.

Sisters of Charity on Trial, Madrid

Even if we are obedient to the gross terms
of black plumage the structure of rain
rains all night. Your baby is not the bird,
birth tray, or empty Spanish swaddle cloth.
Priests pass, are latticed. Your stomach fills
with each hooded crow, sour peels
of crabapple. Take a clean hand. Say it
is not light uncreated. And the sash
of Randy Ryder cradled and stolen in Málaga,
the sun-song in his throat, whom do we lash
and how do we un-paint the nursery?

Pietàs, Cold

Raw bird in no silence.
God on this particular tree.
Pietàs, the kind of tenderness
that plants mercy in the clinic bed.
Hawks arc. The half-acre pears
mean sweet crates of fruit.
Had we seen Spanish infants
in the all-black grass,
the moon coming and coming
like a barrel full of
orchard ends, had we made a hole
for the serviceberry too early
and in our rushing, a canticle
unleashed? There a child
made of rope, there a quiet
fold of green flies. The night
in honor of bound night.

Franco's Stolen Babies

Wait for it—the fat flesh
of infants, their daffodil lids
closed to solid birds outside,
asleep for the seizure of God
to clean their source-wounds,
dragonfly-clear like the blue
dasher on shinleaf.
And how hard is it to soothe
the sun, its overlord
thickness trying to talk nuns
back into piety. All morning
the babies turned up dead,
juniper-curved with
waxy breaths. The damn
faraway birthmothers
slapping their own cheeks.

Network

If it's true that every hour has
its own specific attendant,
you have stayed long enough
with the defected one,
his heart tissue red and
wild mint, and far away the same
trill and trailing grain of sound.
Back and forth a network
of nuns at the hips of new mothers
with their the black knots
hammered sour inside those miracles.
Whatever happens in the verbs
of court sentences I will move
your ankles and wrists to where
sunrise will remake them bone.

Priests, Nuns, Nurses

Nothing will change the seismic
plot, the ether you hear
in each infant wail,
looping each Spanish
stolen baby to Levi,
struggling to lock himself
in the single level house,
pitch spitting
hard from the open stove,
rude shale stuck in
the threads of sunrise.
It will rain. It will rain
with the motion of God.
It will rain pale magnetic
drops and Levi
will suddenly stop
crying and ask about dirt.

He Flung His Arms Around His Face

Levi's floating
the heart of a small washcloth
across the unscrubbed tub,
measuring the wave along the grout
like a lobsterman's eyes too
risen with gulls to ask
about the limits
of plovers and skimmers.
If one makes a pile of birds
one's ghost must light
from that pile. I soap you in
the crosswinds of our farmhouse,
afraid I'll talk you through
the treason of going where
a barefoot girl holds
kinglets with barely a finger.

In the Middle of Good Morning

And the middle of this dry weight
of infants served cold to new mothers,
others on their way to the pale
grounds beyond Santa Cristina Clinic,
in the middle of barberry bluer
than what remains. I can't help
but nurse all the mangled
babies divided into foliage, those
of shorter twilight
and nautical dawn, the ones without combs.
In the middle of finding
my way back to the deaf and boneless
autumns when born alive meant
borrowed fields of boxes.

Put in the Santo Celo

In case the great gain of blackbirds
widens your hips or nuns leave
the birth room with the scarlet flair
of your firstborn. In case the God-play
and lacework of quail is really
the particular haunt of the hawthorn
steady in its weary, I still want
this glass earth to sound.
Skim of hawk heavy in poplars,
yellow birds young and cold
and beginning to feel it,
the quiet circle of law, poppies
pinned and knotted by aster.

Lutalica

There's a field that replaces the sequence
of chipping sparrow calls with something less
than drift and pitch, the incensed loops
of feeding gone wrong, gone Spanish
on a terrace where some new mother has paid
for raw shoulders and neck, a stolen pound of
thorn and breast, light as bag of trillium
or clearweed. Here is where I give no sound.
The earth violet, tight and ditch-filled.
The story of a dandelion on the tibia
of someone else's baby.

Uncle Mengele

I dressed Levi in wool this holiday but thought
about "Uncle Mengele"—needle in hand, sex
organs of one twin on the fat silver table.
I imagined Levi's neck, ten cubic centimeters
of blood drawn daily or typhus shot
into his smooth spine. How wholly the acorns
and birch do nothing amid the red mind. It's almost
snowing. Some twins are stabbed with a thin
needle directly to the heart. Sometimes the mother
is kept alive to keep them from misbehaving
beyond the ramp, her blackbirds
who alabaster into the next canticle.

II

That Our Beauties Should Have Night Terrors

Today is a heavy place, red verdict of
leaves cloven, larch and sugars of pitch,
the babes of Spain gone missing
so blue here in this quail-path,
nearly dripping with wounds of sky
like dull silkworms or infants sold
to flutter, dead asleep in prams,
so cold in their orbiting even nurses
and hungry nuns will not wipe winter
from under their arms. The boy between
Barcelona and Madrid, who is he
but thirst not yet rained upon, blessing
the other beauties bleeding in wet diapers.

Bless Those As We Stare Them into Domes

Of everything plural between us, verdigris
beribboned like a beautifully amputated
God in a Sunday service, the angel's clean
hand a sort of doll's arm the wind takes whole,
only a little violence in that action of green.
Levi says late at night, I love being home—
his high lavish vowels as December fibers
of all glacial infants tightly curled in Spanish
freezers, cooing dead or fully born, moaning
for me, for whatever I cannot bring.

Birthed of Ghosts, 1950–1980

In the weary Junes, priests
performing godless acts on
swaddled muscles, infants
in their slow cardiac simmer,
summers with too much hair
on my neck, lemon rinds in
bushes cut only for the sun
to rot, the unburied children
crying hard for order, and yet
thou art not there, will not hush.
I'll eat the flies the angel
left behind, the sour milk
in a deviled language spoken
only as salvia with quail.

Levi's Bicuspid Valve

In cooperation with loam
and double sweet williams,
Rome apples and borders
of blacksmith cinders first
in shade then spade-deep earth,
slight covering of straw,
trumpet flowers
bringing cleared beds to scarlet,
the whole fruit in a bearing state,
the green fig and Madonna fig
against the utmost, the terms
among themselves.

Franquismo

What else could they do but turn coal-scented
in the nursery, tiny firekeepers oblong
with their awe and sapwood lips, fat cells
of rain and oak flush against the place
I've seen you go—into lean canticles,
into the crowded cypress, sons of mothers
in storerooms and kitchen bags,
Franco's freezer-babies like a pack
of Brueghel's hounds. O' wintered infants,
I should be able to come to thee.
I should be able to wash you with white
soap, soft butter. Scour you back
to the beyond-ice, breathing like winter
gone lithe with the impossibly lemon sun.

Spanish Cold Kiss

It's happening again, a Spanish
cold-kiss, the small lake of
hospital freezers delayed
with newborns, the solid one
nuns bring bedside, already blue
and migrating toward faint geese.
And here the snowdrops
blooming twice since February.
You cannot stop gravity, I tell Levi.
Like you cannot stop the sun, he says.
This is already a long-dead moment,
a project with its own dusk.
Hair green and thick islanded
in this ice, the way we, dear
god, with our enlarged hearts
must smell like a yield of
alfalfa unspirited by the cut.

For Manoli Pagador in Getafe

I bought yours from a priest,
from a batch of three-hundred
thousand, Dr. Vela with his metal
crucifix, baby graves with their stones
over Spanish stones. Nurses
show you how the new dead are—
but birds never lift from their pink
mouths and the only dove that
circles is from a flock of black.

Franco in the Blood

Motherfucking babies, blue on the frozen tray, nominal at rest
in their first recline, blue spooling around them light as
heavenly fog. Here are the fields we threaten to sell
for maples, their sap the grandeur
of what we call being autumn
to our firstborns, their pewter hearts growing large.
Because I saw your birth, I am responsible for all the dead.

Almanac of the Terrible Flowers
(after Merwin)

It's Levi who brings me
to you stolen Spanish tots
alone in your great
metal cribs breathing
called away carried by
the wrong nurses through
each corridor fresh
into the dead manna
of terraced grapes
these vows the heavy
bread-scent of your wrists
your clean
breath of vowels
God alone in his
longing for geese
this is how it becomes
two chances this is how
you could have been
lifted from the beginning
of leaves into the palms
of large nuns waking
next October to a new
mother with flesh-red
flowers outside

Hylomorphism

Late splice of sunflowers, owls
then no owls in the silver life
of blue grass. O' the structure
of wrath decades after the sobering
tools, pairs of toddlers spread
low in smoke-sun, in the bid
for spleen, liver, sex organs
and the cheeks of some risen boy,
not even bone but the territory
of bone, the sacrosanct details
either bronzed or burned.

Levi Incarnate

In the falling of snow geese
you come back from digging,
cooled by blasts of April
through barberry,
your thin voice with pollen,
like the true cold of
babies kept for Franco's nuns.
It's not for baptism now that I pour
water on the cowlick of your
high-wheat hair, you in the hedges
of language gone feral, locked in arcs
of purple-voiced calls.
In the tantrum-heavy damp
you could be Spanish and I could
be your new Spanish mother, together
we could be psalm, pulse.

The Open Poem

The way to launch a bird-bone
into winter air is
to pretend it is a biplane
a toddler's glider
your dead mother's charm
bracelet so it catches on
branches keeps its sway
so the empty cells of snow
might reach the silver
of its loyal footballs
and lucky hearts
the way to launch anything
halved into angel-rich rain
is to stand and stand and stay
standing the way stolen babies
might wait to watch the trials
of nuns and priests, doctors
in the open poem of leaving
the body for a single cardinal

Like Slate Beneath Virgin's Bower

In rain we miss the shadblow
and sumac, wide hemlock damask and
warped in its own silver balding,
the way babies of Franco's nuns
must have not died in their swaddle
cloths in the Spanish enclave of Melilla
in Morocco where infants were harvested
like cork oak, or slate beneath virgin's bower.
Like any mother I wait in the green,
slaked by nothing but the visible architecture
of distant November when sounds from the throat
are holy as tiny granite lips returning.

Breath

I made you to know what no angel
knows in its whirlwind blood-love,
unblackening on this page
of violet snow, in charge of nothing
but beading itself on that branch
where pears are less liable to fall.
I made you to read this now,
heels crossed, willowed in
the architecture of following
an echo to no central heart.
Spanish babies stolen—I am sorry
to say I never saw the sun seed
this earthing, the poppies with wounds
blooming, a field where the last crow
increases into pewter weight.

Quietus

Who, after all, will find us?
In the case of Carmen Martinez
there were no grave or nativity
records, each time her sac would break
she'd sleep through the abduction.
What by-products, those ice-babies
who never actually turned blue.
Levi, when you play fire trucks
and police ambulances I am worn
and punctured in a tangled place,
full of clean hazel loam, lost
in the ghazal-force of rain.
Small sticks, let them be planted.
Rendered for another nursery.

Freezer Trays

If there's a way to write you
out of stillbirth fiction and
freezer trays, surely we must settle
such sounds, mothers inflammable
as when birds lie down in the
colors that made them, their clutch
upon me like Flamenco blood,
baby blue haunted things so perfect
in this rain, violated by bright
trees that will confess anything
with enough wind. The nuns have
been leaving again in the ether
and underflush of birthings,
selecting naval and nose,
mosaic canticle of lung-sounds.
Heaven is so soiled with theft
no mother can pray.

III

With Water

Is there a trail home?
The geese aren't hungry
for our thoughts, locked in
their long true flight.
The way Dr. Vela
presses a metal crucifix
to one journalist's face,
the foul solace of his crime
public as camp robbers
on safflower seed.
Imagine Levi's twilight
mouth, his flurried
switch grass tongue on the
far waist of another mother.
It's not a question you can
answer with water, the water
is nothing but priests.

God in the Ground

One true thing is Manuela Polo
has found her daughter.
All these years the oily blood
of Spanish afternoons,
newborns in fresh clothes
landbound toward God
in the ground, though the
the whitest green sky,
the white-livered quail.
Though over the sound
of being born is the slide
of bindweed earth.
Six pounds of chicory
is love nonetheless.

The Fuller Act of Wailing

There's something wrong
with the earth again
the silent lie that is
warehouse to juniper
cult of hot weather
surge of Spanish infants
weighed and sold
as dumb stones
in the village of
Castrillo de Murcia
or somewhere
in the blue tiles
of Madrid and how
do we great as any soul
of scrub jays
devil the topsoil
clot any birth
in festival

A Way of Making April

Wet dawn. Loose, self-portrait
wind. Snowmen with mosquitos
and carrots. Trying for a custody of
the eyes and failing. I've chased green
stars around Spanish clinics,
green thunderclouds into the whole
absorption of bitters. This is an apology
in the middle of a field of soaking barley.
Umbrage of nuns and nurses
in the dove-caught arches of April.
If it has taken me this long to find
the newborns' flexed tendons,
if a condition of the heart is weighted
descent, I am sorry. We are abandoned
even if we remember the blackbirds.

Nurse

God help that mother
whose swollen dead love
is being washed
waiting for the warm box
made of hell
knows what kind of wood
and there it will worm
in muscled patchwork
become branchlets bluets
blushing red meat
odorless for no one
and in the third year
it will ripen more
in the third year it will breathe
the sharp October
the air with bidens and
alder and that my dear
is how it will nurse

Occhiolism

With our lips, with a clearer custody of
our eyes, I say we end the long sentence
here with the daffodil on the stone
joints of newborns. The blue details
of perfection are but plain jays
come forth for mixed seed. Both in fable
and fact there is a rock in every landscape.
This is a common, common field.
I am only the sackcloth of a mother.

The High Will

O' Sister Maria Gomez, there are more
infants taken from the dry fibers
of mothers. Before dawn, I walk Levi
to birds treated kindly to death,
asleep in snow. It's generous, I tell him
to be bound by a spine so blue
the high clouds will shine the whole
scoured flock, each March body
the great utility of law lifted from law,
in the regular sun and bitter after.

My Sleep Wasn't

My sleep wasn't a bonfire
of infants, it was only me
still afraid of God's
particular muck
the salt of birth
no richer than birth
the intrinsic value of
bones weighing next
to nothing in May
any kind of cypress
that moves by hands
of weather sounds of
Iniesta and Olaya
and Alcalde vowels
are what happen
at the end of pain

Radio Te Encontraré

What is there to say on air,
the rattling that came from God
went straight to my son and
yours, I will be friendly if we
shall meet, I will bring
bread with raw almonds,
soft cheese like brie, so small
elegant us, made of green
syllables and an error of fury.

Apace, or the Sound of Good Grasses

Morning, full of freed
hawks and sketchpad birds,
derivative finch and varied thrush
in the cheap tablet of dawn.
I go to the window and learn
nothing but birdseed and mailbox.
Small is not the beauty whose name
I forego, not this flyover
prairie gently wounded with wheat.
In shotgun light we eat fresh berries
and cheese like a wandering lot
holding viburnum without bloom,
already black, all together common.

The Priest's Freezer

There's not just one beast
in every yellow canticle.
Little ones kicking at nuns
or hung in the priest's freezer.
Water is only awe and golden
glands of infants. The earth is
easy to wash and the sun can
retard any dead wisdom.
But this cry, this tiny
fatty cry becomes what
I cannot carry to mouth.

True Ribs

What now? The blue infants
still want to sing. The absolute
debt of true ribs is shoved
right here in the sugary wind.
What is the right thing
to say to the red water?
The Judas, snowdrop and
fringe trees will grow ripe
but may not rise until
the second spring. Even
marigold is kin if kin
is questioned under oath.

Previous titles in the Carnegie Mellon Poetry Series

Shinemaster, Michael McFee
Eastern Mountain Time, Joyce Peseroff
Dragging the Lake, Robert Thomas

2007
Trick Pear, Suzanne Cleary
So I Will Till the Ground, Gregory Djanikian
Black Threads, Jeff Friedman
Drift and Pulse, Kathleen Halme
The Playhouse Near Dark, Elizabeth Holmes
On the Vanishing of Large Creatures, Susan Hutton
One Season Behind, Sarah Rosenblatt
Indeed I Was Pleased with the World, Mary Ruefle
The Situation, John Skoyles

2008
The Grace of Necessity, Samuel Green
After West, James Harms
Anticipate the Coming Reservoir, John Hoppenthaler
Convertible Night, Flurry of Stones, Dzvinia Orlowsky
Parable Hunter, Ricardo Pau-Llosa
The Book of Sleep, Eleanor Stanford

2009
Divine Margins, Peter Cooley
Cultural Studies, Kevin A. González
Dear Apocalypse, K. A. Hays
Warhol-o-rama, Peter Oresick
Cave of the Yellow Volkswagen, Maureen Seaton
Group Portrait from Hell, David Schloss
Birdwatching in Wartime, Jeffrey Thomson

2010
The Diminishing House, Nicky Beer
A World Remembered, T. Alan Broughton
Say Sand, Daniel Coudriet
Knock Knock, Heather Hartley
In the Land We Imagined Ourselves, Jonathan Johnson

Selected Early Poems: 1958-1983, Greg Kuzma
The Other Life: Selected Poems, Herbert Scott
Admission, Jerry Williams

2011
Having a Little Talk with Capital P Poetry, Jim Daniels
Oz, Nancy Eimers
Working in Flour, Jeff Friedman
Scorpio Rising: Selected Poems, Richard Katrovas
The Politics, Benjamin Paloff
Copperhead, Rachel Richardson

2012
Now Make an Altar, Amy Beeder
Still Some Cake, James Cummins
Comet Scar, James Harms
Early Creatures, Native Gods, K. A. Hays
That Was Oasis, Michael McFee
Blue Rust, Joseph Millar
Spitshine, Anne Marie Rooney
Civil Twilight, Margot Schilpp

2013
Oregon, Henry Carlile
Selvage, Donna Johnson
At the Autopsy of Vaslav Nijinksy, Bridget Lowe
Silvertone, Dzvinia Orlowsky
Fibonacci Batman: New & Selected Poems (1991-2011),
        Maureen Seaton
When We Were Cherished, Eve Shelnutt
The Fortunate Era, Arthur Smith
Birds of the Air, David Yezzi

2014
Night Bus to the Afterlife, Peter Cooley
Alexandria, Jasmine Bailey
Dear Gravity, Gregory Djanikian
Pretenders, Jeff Friedman

How I Went Red, Maggie Glover
All That Might Be Done, Samuel Green
Man, Ricardo Pau-Llosa
The Wingless, Cecilia Llompart

2015
The Octopus Game, Nicky Beer
The Voices, Michael Dennis Browne
Domestic Garden, John Hoppenthaler
We Mammals in Hospitable Times, Jynne Dilling Martin
And His Orchestra, Benjamin Paloff
Know Thyself, Joyce Peseroff
cadabra, Dan Rosenberg
The Long Haul, Vern Rutsala
Bartram's Garden, Eleanor Stanford

2016
Something Sinister, Hayan Charara
The Spokes of Venus, Rebecca Morgan Frank
Adult Swim, Heather Hartley
Swastika into Lotus, Richard Katrovas
The Nomenclature of Small Things, Lynn Pedersen
Hundred-Year Wave, Rachel Richardson
Where Are We in This Story, Sarah Rosenblatt
Inside Job, John Skoyles
Suddenly It's Evening: Selected Poems, John Skoyles

2017
Custody of the Eyes, Kimberly Burwick
Dream of the Gone-From City, Barbara Edelman
Windthrow, K. A. Hays
We Were Once Here, Michael McFee
Kingdom, Joseph Millar
The Histories, Jason Whitmarsh